T0086101

Little People, BIG DREAMS™
KYLIE MINOGUE

Written by
Maria Isabel Sánchez Vegara

Illustrated by
Rebecca Gibbon

Frances Lincoln
Children's Books

Once there was a talented girl in Australia called Kylie. She inherited her love for singing and dancing from her mother, a former ballet dancer. And, by sewing with her grandmother, she also got a taste for fashion.

In class, Kylie was shy and quiet. She never took part in the school plays. But back home, her favorite game was singing for her friends. Using a broom as a microphone, she dreamed of being a star on stage.

Her chance to perform came sooner than expected when her aunt took Kylie and her sister to audition for a small role in a soap opera. When Kylie got in front of the camera, the crew knew she was the actor they were looking for!

Dannii
We love
you!
you ni
xx

AUSTRALIA
POST

Dannii

Dannii

Dannii

Dannii

Dannii

Dannii

Dannii Minogue

Dannii Minogue

Dannii

DANNII

Dannii

But it was her sister, Dannii, who shot to stardom first, singing in a youth talent show on television. Kylie was happy to help her deal with mountains of fan mail, hoping that—one day—she could inspire people, too.

DIRECTOR

She kept auditioning without much luck. Until, aged 17, she landed a main role in "The Henderson Kids." The series gave her a chance to improve her acting skills. Still, even the best actor forgets a line every now and then ...

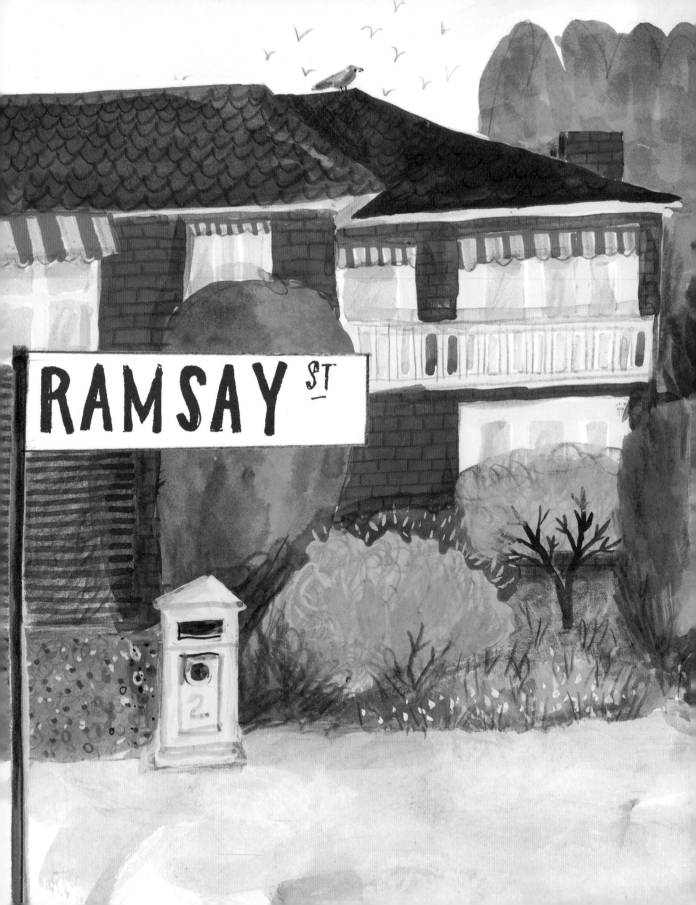

Her character was written out, but it ended up being for the best. Soon, she got a big role in "Neighbours" playing Charlene, a feisty mechanic with a crush on her buddy, Scott. Everyone was hooked on their love story!

"Neighbours" became one of the most beloved soap operas. Yet Kylie hadn't forgotten her passion for music. She recorded an old song and made it sound brand new. It became a sensation in Australia and made Kylie a pop star!

Next, she traveled to London, excited to work at a famous recording studio. Somehow, everyone there had forgotten she was coming. Kylie's new song was written in just 40 minutes, but it ended up being a classic.

Yet, hit after hit, Kylie felt a bit like a puppet in the hands
of her record company. They rarely asked her opinion.
One day, she decided to buy some clothes she loved and wore
them in a video. Expressing herself in her own way felt great!

With every new song, Kylie made pop music fresh again. She experimented with awesome sounds, stunning looks, and spectacular music videos.

The best artists, designers, and directors were thrilled
to work beside her.

Kylie was on tour when doctors told her she had breast cancer. It was a difficult time, yet she shared her journey through the illness, inspiring others to visit their doctor for regular check-ups.

She returned shining brighter than ever! Kylie became the first female artist to have a chart-topping album five decades in a row. From the young to the young at heart, everyone grooved to the rhythm of her songs.

And it was by dazzling the world with her talent, dedication, and love for music that little Kylie turned into the Princess of Pop: a true star who will forever reign over the dance floor.

KYLIE MINOGUE

(Born 1968)

1988

2002

Kylie Ann Minogue grew up in Melbourne, Australia, with her two younger siblings, Dannii and Brendan. She landed her first television role aged eight, appearing in several episodes of the WWII Australian drama series: "The Sullivans." For much of her childhood, Kylie focused on her schoolwork rather than acting. She was seventeen before she won her first lead role, playing Charlotte in "The Henderson Kids." However, her big break was being cast as Charlene in "Neighbours," a popular Australian soap opera. When Kylie's character got married, over twenty-one million people tuned in to watch! After singing at a charity event, she was signed to a record label. With her first song, "The Loco-Motion," she brought the 1962 tune to a whole new audience. She soon decided to leave acting

2006

2019

and follow her love for music. Her first album, titled "Kylie," was a top-ten hit in the UK and Australia. Over the next fifteen years she released eight more albums including the iconic singles: "Better the Devil You Know," "Spinning Around," and "Can't Get You Out of My Head." In 2005, she was diagnosed with breast cancer during her "Showgirl" world tour. After successful treatment and rest, she returned to the stage. Kylie is passionate about raising breast cancer awareness, supports many children's charities, and is a proud ally of the LGBTQ+ community. Her 2023 single, "Padam Padam," quickly became a Pride anthem. She has also headlined Glastonbury festival and launched a Las Vegas residency. Whatever Kylie does, she never fails to wow her millions of fans across the world!

Want to find out more?

Have a read of this great book:

A History of Music for Children
by Mary Richards, David Schweitzer, and Rose Blake

With help from an adult, you can watch Kylie's amazing performances online.

Published by Peter Marley · Designed by Sasha Moxon
Commissioned by Lucy Menzies · Edited by Molly Mead
Production by Nikki Ingram

Manufactured in Guangdong, China CC122023
1 3 5 7 9 8 6 4 2

Photographic acknowledgments (pages 28-29, from left to right): 1. Australian pop singer and actress Kylie Minogue in her role
as Charlene in the Australian soap opera Neighbours February 1988 © Trinity Mirror/Mirrorpix via Alamy Stock Photo. 2. Kylie
Minogue performing 'Can't Get You Out of My Head' during The 22nd BRIT Awards Show, Earls Court 2, London, UK, Wednesday
20 February 2002 © JMEnternational via Getty Images. 3. Kylie Minogue, in feather and sequins, returned to the stage for her
'Homecoming' concert, after an 18 month fight against breast cancer, 11th November 2006 SHD Picture by Dallas Kilponen ©
Fairfax Media via Getty Images. 4. Glastonbury, Pilton, Somerset, UK. 30th June 2019. Kylie Minogue performs on the Pyramid stage
at Glastonbury Festival on 30th June 2019. Picture by Tabatha Fireman © Female Perspective via Alamy Stock Photo.

Collect the Little People, BIG DREAMS™ series:

FRIDA KAHLO	COCO CHANEL	MAYA ANGELOU	AMELIA EARHART	AGATHA CHRISTIE	MARIE CURIE	ROSA PARKS	AUDREY HEPBURN	EMMELINE PANKHURST
ELLA FITZGERALD	ADA LOVELACE	JANE AUSTEN	GEORGIA O'KEEFFE	HARRIET TUBMAN	ANNE FRANK	MOTHER TERESA	JOSEPHINE BAKER	L. M. MONTGOMERY
JANE GOODALL	SIMONE DE BEAUVOIR	MUHAMMAD ALI	STEPHEN HAWKING	MARIA MONTESSORI	VIVIENNE WESTWOOD	MAHATMA GANDHI	DAVID BOWIE	WILMA RUDOLPH
DOLLY PARTON	BRUCE LEE	RUDOLF NUREYEV	ZAHA HADID	MARY SHELLEY	MARTIN LUTHER KING JR.	DAVID ATTENBOROUGH	ASTRID LINDGREN	EVONNE GOOLAGONG
BOB DYLAN	ALAN TURING	BILLIE JEAN KING	GRETA THUNBERG	JESSE OWENS	JEAN-MICHEL BASQUIAT	ARETHA FRANKLIN	CORAZON AQUINO	PELÉ
ERNEST SHACKLETON	STEVE JOBS	AYRTON SENNA	LOUISE BOURGEOIS	ELTON JOHN	JOHN LENNON	PRINCE	CHARLES DARWIN	CAPTAIN TOM MOORE
HANS CHRISTIAN ANDERSEN	STEVIE WONDER	MEGAN RAPINOE	MARY ANNING	MALALA YOUSAFZAI	ANDY WARHOL	RUPAUL	MICHELLE OBAMA	MINDY KALING